Celebrations!
Wesak

Anita Ganeri

Heinemann

H www.heinemann.co.uk/library
Visit our website to find out more information about Heinemann Library books.

To order:
☎ Phone 44 (0) 1865 888066
📄 Send a fax to 44 (0) 1865 314091
🖥 Visit the Heinemann Bookshop at www.heinemann.co.uk/library to browse our catalogue and order online.

First published in Great Britain by Heinemann Library,
Halley Court, Jordan Hill, Oxford OX2 8EJ
a division of Reed Educational and Professional Publishing Ltd.
Heinemann is a registered trademark of Reed Educational & Professional Publishing Ltd.

OXFORD MELBOURNE AUCKLAND
JOHANNESBURG BLANTYRE GABORONE
IBADAN PORTSMOUTH (NH) USA CHICAGO

© Reed Educational and Professional Publishing Ltd 2002
The moral right of the proprietor has been asserted.

Designed by Celia Floyd
Originated by Ambassador Litho Ltd   500 757675
Printed by Wing King Tong in Hong Kong

ISBN 0 431 13792 7 (hardback)   ISBN 0 431 13800 1 (paperback)
06 05 04 03 02   06 05 04 03 02
10 9 8 7 6 5 4 3 2   10 9 8 7 6 5 4 3 2 1

British Library Cataloguing in Publication Data

Ganeri, Anita
  Wesak. – (Celebrations)
  1. Wesak – Juvenile literature
  I. Title
  394.2'6534

Acknowledgements
The Publishers would like to thank the following for permission to reproduce photographs:
Andes Press Agency: Carlos Reyes-Manzo pp12, 13, 14, 15, 16; Ann and Bury Peerless: pp6, 7; Chris Schwartz: p19; Circa Photo Library: William Holtby p20; Don Farber: p21; Corbis: Richard Bickel p4, Christine Osborne p5, Luca I Tettoni p8, Alison Wright p9, Brian Vikander p10, Chris Lisle p11; Robert Harding Picture Library: David Beatty p18

Cover photograph reproduced with permission of Andes Press Agency: Carlos Reyes Manzo

Our thanks to the Bradford Interfaith Education Centre for their comments in the preparation of this book.

Every effort has been made to contact copyright holders of any material reproduced in this book. Any omissions will be rectified in subsequent printings if notice is given to the Publisher.

Contents

Words printed in **bold letters like these** are explained in the glossary.

The Buddha's birthday

The **Buddhist** festival of Wesak (Vesak) happens in April or May. It is a very important time for Buddhists. This is when many Buddhists celebrate three special events. These are the **Buddha**'s birthday, his **enlightenment** and his **passing away**. The Buddha was a man who lived in India about 2500 years ago. Buddhists follow his teachings as a guide for their lives. Wesak is also called Buddha Day.

A huge statue of the Buddha in Burma.

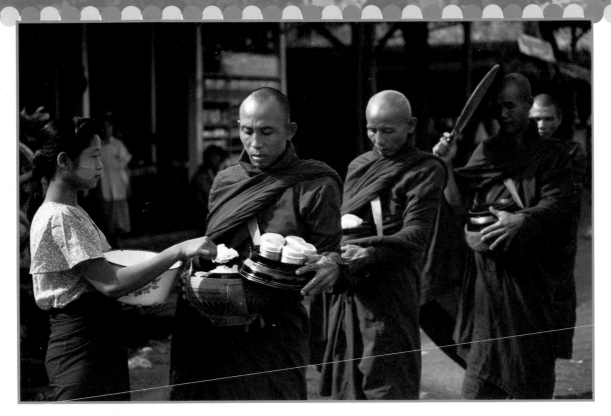

Monks in Burma receive food at Wesak.

At Wesak, Buddhists remember the Buddha's teachings. They try to be especially kind and generous to others, as the Buddha taught. Some decorate their homes and send Wesak cards to their friends. Some also visit their local temple or centre to pay their respects to the Buddha and to give gifts to the **monks**.

In Buddhist countries, people celebrate Wesak on the full moon day of April or May. They believe that the most important times in the Buddha's life happened on full moon days. In Britain, Buddhists celebrate Wesak on the nearest weekend.

The story of the Buddha

Buddhists follow the teachings of a man called **Siddattha Gotama**. He became the **Buddha**. According to the story, Siddattha was an Indian prince. He was born about 2500 years ago in Lumbini in Nepal. When Siddattha was born, a wise man came to visit his father, the king. He told him that when his son grew up he would become a great king or a great teacher.

This is Lumbini in Nepal, birthplace of the Buddha.

Siddattha grew up in his father's luxurious palace. He had everything he wanted. Then, one day, he went out riding. While he was out, he saw an old man, a sick man and the funeral of a dead man. He was horrified. He had never seen people suffer before. Then he saw a **holy** man, dressed in simple robes. The holy man had given up everything he owned. But he seemed very happy. Siddattha decided to be like him. That night, he left the palace and began his search for an end to unhappiness.

Siddattha sees four new sights when he leaves his father's palace.

Siddattha and the evil one

For six years, the story says, **Siddattha Gotama** lived in the forest with a group of **holy** men. It was a very hard life. They ate and drank almost nothing. Soon Siddattha looked like a skeleton. But still he did not find the answers he was looking for.

Siddattha sitting under the **bodhi tree** (see next page).

One day, he left the forest and made his way to a village called Bodh Gaya. He sat down under a tall tree and began to **meditate**. All day and night, he sat there. During the night, **Mara**, the evil one tried to make Siddattha give up his search. Mara tried to seize the ground Siddattha was sitting on. But Siddattha calmly put out his hand and touched the ground. An earthquake shook and Mara fled in terror.

Buddhists meditating under a bodhi tree.

Then Siddattha, at last, gained **enlightenment**. It was like a light going on in the darkness. Suddenly he knew why suffering happened and how it could be stopped. From then on, he became the **Buddha**.

The Buddha's teachings

After his **enlightenment**, the **Buddha** went to a peaceful deer park and gave his first talk. The reason people suffered, he said, was that they always wanted what they could not have. They always wanted more. He taught them to follow a path that would lead to an end to suffering. This meant leading a good life, being kind and caring, and training your mind to see things in the right way.

This wheel stands for the Buddha's teachings.

A stone carving of the Buddha who passed away lying on his side.

The Buddha spent the rest of his life travelling around India and teaching people how to live. He and his followers lived as **monks**. Many people came to join them. There was even a terrible robber who heard the Buddha and gave up his wicked ways. The Buddha **passed away** (**Buddhists** do not say he died), when he was 80 years old. Just before he passed away, he told his monks not to be sad. They must carry on his teaching after him.

The Three Jewels

The Buddha, his teaching and the family of Buddhists are called the Three Jewels. Buddhists say that they are precious and beautiful, just like jewels.

Visiting the temple

At Wesak, many **Buddhists** decorate their homes with lamps and flowers. Light is very important for Buddhists. It lights up the darkness just as the **Buddha**'s teachings light up their lives. Some people send Wesak cards to their friends. Some people give each other little gifts, such as flowers, candles or sticks of **incense**.

A girl with some flowers for Wesak.

Wesak cards

Try making your own Wesak card. Decorate it with a picture of the Buddha or of a **lotus flower** or a **bodhi tree**. Write 'Happy Wesak' inside.

Many Buddhists visit their local temple or centre to join the **monks** and their friends in a day of celebration. Many dress in simple, white clothes for the day. Wesak is a time for being especially generous so people take gifts of food for the monks. They also help prepare and serve a Wesak meal which is shared by everyone. Many Buddhists are **vegetarians** because they do not believe in killing animals to eat. The meal might include curries, rice, salads and fruit. There is water, fruit juice and tea to drink.

Buddhists at a London temple on Wesak Day.

Honouring the Buddha

A very important part of Wesak is honouring the **Buddha**. This is called **puja**. **Buddhists** do not **worship** the Buddha as a god. They honour him as a great teacher. In the temple, people take off their shoes and go into the **shrine** room. They sit or kneel in front of a beautiful image of the Buddha. The image reminds people of the Buddha's teaching.

A Buddhist shrine decorated for Wesak.

People join the **monks** in chanting verses from the **holy** books and remembering the Three Jewels. Then they place offerings of flowers, candles and **incense** on the shrine in front of the Buddha. Each of the offerings has a special meaning. The flowers look lovely but they will soon die. This reminds people that nothing lasts for ever. The sweet smell of incense is like the sweetness of the Buddha's teaching.

Children honouring the Buddha at Wesak.

For Buddhists, being kind and caring is very important, especially at Wesak time. As part of the Wesak puja, they promise to follow the Buddha's teachings, not to harm living things, to tell the truth and to be patient and helpful.

Stories and plays

There is plenty for **Buddhist** children to do at Wesak. They listen to talks by the **monks** about what Wesak means. In some temples and centres, children act out a play about the **Buddha**'s life. A favourite play is the story of wicked **Mara** and how he tries to harm the Buddha (see page 9).

A Buddhist monk talking to children at Wesak.

At Wesak, children listen to stories about the Buddha. These are called **Jataka** stories. In these stories, the Buddha often appears as an animal to teach a lesson. In one story, the Buddha was born as a wise hare. He was willing to give up everything he had for the sake of others. This teaches children the importance of sharing. Other stories help them to understand about helping others and making friends.

Animal masks

Act out one of the Jataka stories with your friends. Make masks out of card for some of the animals. You could choose a hare, a lion or an elephant.

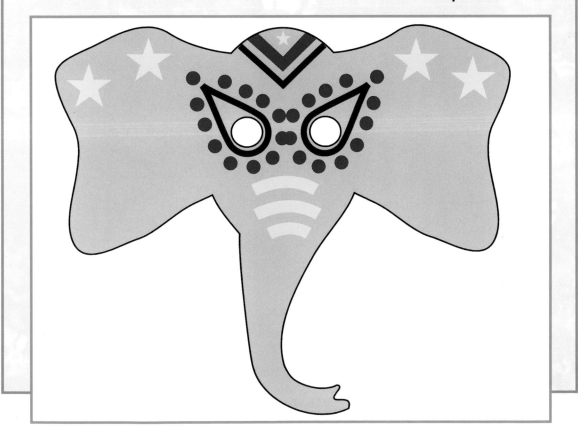

Around the world

In many **Buddhist** countries, Wesak is the most popular festival of the year. In Sri Lanka, people decorate their homes and temples with lights. Huge decorations showing scenes from the **Buddha**'s life light up the streets. These lights remind people of the Buddha's **enlightenment** and of the light they can find if they follow his teaching. People also make special Wesak

lanterns from paper stuck over a wooden frame. In the temple, they place rings of little lamps around the **bodhi tree**.

Paper lanterns at a Buddhist festival in Sri Lanka.

A very important part of Buddhist life is being generous to other people. At Wesak, Buddhists visit the temple with gifts of food for the **monks**. They believe that this will help them on their own journey to enlightenment. The monks do not ask for food. People are happy to give it. Buddhists also spend time **meditating**. This means clearing your mind so that it is calm and peaceful. People sit cross-legged on the floor, close their eyes and breathe calmly and evenly. It takes a lot of practice.

Buddhists meditating in Sri Lanka.

Remembering the Buddha

In Thailand, **Buddhists** visit the temple at Wesak to pay their respects. A special part of the celebration is pouring perfumed water over the image of the **Buddha**. This reminds them of the Buddha's birthday when the gods bathed him with sweet-smelling water. Then they walk three times clockwise around the temple. This reminds them of the Three Jewels. These are the Buddha, his teachings and the Buddhist family.

Washing the Buddha in Thailand at Wesak.

Wherever they live in the world, Buddhists remember the important times in the Buddha's life. Some remember his birthday, **enlightenment** and **passing away** at Wesak. Others remember his enlightenment but mark his birthday and passing away on different days.

These are happy times when people try especially hard to live up to the Buddha's teachings and follow in his footsteps.

Lights are placed on a temple in Thailand as people celebrate the Buddha's teachings.

Buddhist festival calendar

There are many different groups of **Buddhists**. Some have their own festivals. The festivals below are celebrated by the group called Theravada Buddhists. They mainly come from Sri Lanka, Burma and Thailand. Some live in Britain. There are also many British people who have become followers of Theravada Buddhism.

February	Magha **Puja** (Remembers the **Buddha**'s teachings to his **monks** just before he **passed away**)
April	Songkran (New Year in Thailand)
April/May	Wesak/Buddha Day (Remembers the Buddha's birthday, **enlightenment** and passing away)
June/July	Poson (Remembers how Buddhism came to Sri Lanka)
July/August	Asala/Dharma Day (Remembers the Buddha's first teaching in Sarnath, India)
October/ November	Kathina (Buddhists give gifts of new robes to the monks)
November	Loi Kratong (The festival of lights in Thailand)

Glossary

bodhi tree tree underneath which the Buddha sat and gained enlightenment

Buddha name given to Siddattha Gotama after his enlightenment. It means the 'enlightened one'.

Buddhist person who follows the teachings of the Buddha

enlightenment seeing and understanding the truth

holy to do with God or a religious teacher

incense stick or block that is burned and makes a sweet smell

Jataka story about one of the Buddha's past lives. The Buddha often appears as an animal.

lotus flower plant that lives in rivers and ponds. It is special to Buddhists.

Mara evil one who tries to make the Buddha give up his search for the truth

meditate to clear your mind so that you feel calm and relaxed

monk man who gives up his home and belongings to devote himself to a way of life or a religion

passing away death of the Buddha

puja the way Buddhists worship the Buddha by offering flowers, candles and incense at a shrine

shrine very holy place

Siddattha Gotama the Buddha's name before his enlightenment

vegetarian person who does not eat meat

worship to show love and respect to God or a great teacher

Index

24